THE SIN OF FEEDING WILD BIRDS

The Sin

of

Feeding Wild Birds

Poems

Logan Garner

BROKEN TRIBE PRESS

The Sin of Feeding Wild Birds

Copyright © 2025 Logan Garner
First Edition

Paperback ISBN: 9781965412114

Cover art and design by Jacob Arms

Published by Broken Tribe Press
Lawrence Landing Company
Raleigh, North Carolina 27609
USA, North America

Broken Tribe Press is a proud member of:

Independent Book Publishers Association
 and
Community of Literary Magazines and Presses

www.brokentribepress.com

BROKEN TRIBE PRESS

CONTENTS

Acknowledgments and Credits

MEZUZAH

The tallest cedar
In Olympic National Forest
A peninsula's ancient crown
Finally toppled

I tore from her flesh
The length of my arm
A proportion and part
Of the fallen whole
To fasten raw on the wall:
Wordless bastardized mezuzah
Blaspheming
Blessing
Wilding my home

Quinault Wilderness, WA

CORRIDOR

Shuffling bent like a windswept surf pine
and leaning gasping just so
against taupe corridor wallpaper—
two dozen doors to either side,
each watching still and stolid—
the old man strains to pick up
his dropped keycard to the tiny
amenity-free room.

It may as well be miles down.

I pass him, feel the tug
of shame, compassion, dignity
and turn back to help him retrieve
the distant plastic, to reach his own
allotted door where he huffs and labors
stepping small into the room
with the too-loud television to muffle
his cries if he falls in there.

I leave him to himself, to his time,
and turn to make for the front desk
to ask them if they might
check on him in the morning.

I stop and stand and breathe
for a time between taupe walls
and turn toward my room without word
to them, to him, to my wife
about the fear.

HERE, IN THE FLOODPLAIN

Here in the floodplain where
sand dominates the soil
we grow wildflowers and
sit on red bricks,

spines bent over books while a
pig and some dogs push
their noses around our
tiny plot of land.

The house has been settling, too.
Cinders slight downward with
every hundred passes
of trucked tons of earth
from down the street where
a big box store will be.

You can roll a marble
south to northwest on our kitchen floor
as reliably as you can find
the round desiccated things
that journeyed beneath
the refrigerator, and

seeds of small, hidden projects
which threaten to grow into
expensive realities
of pine and copper
and steel and plywood.

At eight feet above the
sea and not more than a
crow-flying mile from the
compulsive waves, we get
to feel a part.

Right outside our door, when
the wind carries a faint drone
whispering salt
or, when it rains angry

and the tide is in,
watertable riding high,
we sit and look
at the moat in the yard.

That's when we (and a pig
and some dogs) all
cloister ourselves,
each in our own space, to nest
and burrow and close our eyes
for a time.

THE SIN OF FEEDING WILD BIRDS

The sin of feeding wild birds
might be forgiven by some winter solstice god
if only you can find that one scrub jay
who—upon discovering the peanuts
you've cast into the yard like
broken and shameful acts
into tall, yellowed, damp grass
—who hides them only meters away
under blades all rushing to rot
in reliable winter rains
which somehow last months
and which subsist on hidden dreams
of long-dead summer days
and failed ventures of silly jays.

BLANK VERSE SONNET

In the afternoon I made us hummus,
rinsed out the dregs of the finished product—
an impromptu broth for potato soup—
was elated at the revelation.
The pan rustique that I had overbaked
was transmogrified into herbed croutons.
The next loaf, which I salvaged, just barely,
would become a shared bread bowl for us both.
It felt like that day before your birthday
when I discovered the tchotchke trinket
to add to your amalgamated gift
like a piece I didn't know was missing
which made the loving jigsaw-image whole
that I'd been out to conjure from the start.

GENUFLECTION

The plucking of a single
red huckleberry—wild
beyond your or my cultivation—
to set on a virgin nurse log
while the Swainson's thrush
drips, drips,
drips honeyed whispers,
invisible in the brush.
Amen.

HATCHET MAN

Her nest of hair rides high and gray and wily,
not so much from style as a lack.
Both it and she are unfettered
by qualm or care,
free and easy as wind chimes
of retired green glass bottles.

Even her convictions are winds
blustering northerly or southerly
with mood or circumstance.

On some nights she finds her way
to a basement cafe all twilit by low watt edisons,
a skin-oil patina on the bar, and,
swaying from one intoxicant or another,
takes in the dark tempos of
rare and mundane words alike.

Tonight there's a man her junior by years
yet no spring chicken, no step-spring left.

He's got his own gray and wily thing going on,
reminding witnesses that looks
aren't for much besides looking
and that low clouds carry
more shade than rain.

Only actions, the man says, and promises kept
speak to value and character.
And he is here speaking his.

And there, he goes on thrumming,
drum-kicks on the floor with his heel
chomping out syllables and chopping
at the air with an open palm
like a Hudson Bay ax
splitting and spitting truth
into splintered words that rhyme
but do little else.

5 NOVEMBER

You called me.

Sam—the dog
—our sweet boy
was gone.

Come home, he's a pile
under the kitchen table.
His late final den.

The food we ordered some days later,
after another hours-long cry,
was deep fried, crusted thick,
figurative ash caking
the soft palates of our mouths.

Today we drive
to take a walk, just us,
mosquitoes nitpicking
and reeling close.
Your arms crossed.
My head down.

The surf pines all lean
together over us, rude and low
up over the dunes.
Here's the tide rolling in dark
beneath the gray and climbing anvils.

We're coming into some weather.

BLUE LIGHT

There.
Let your eyes unfocus a little.
Do you see it?
Glimmering just past the tree line,
a stone's throw inside the woods.

A visitor, I think,
from another place.
A neighbor from
somewhere over there,
or perhaps neither.
Perhaps some technology;
a casing of glass and wire.
Or some phosphorescent thing,
mundane and natural.

But I don't think so.

I only glimpse it when I'm up
late at night on restless feet,
trying to lose my way in a
ten by twelve space,
only to pass that same tree
again and again at my kitchen window.

Or when old arguments
resurrected by careless words
leave me chewing and working
my tired jaw, tight throat
unable to swallow them back down.

It comes.

TELEOLOGY OF THE SOIL

Struck from flight by a single still wire,
polyester line pulled taught,
and the wing crumpled.
The shuddering body roared, far from
any eyes or ears and above any
pitch heard by us; a perfectly silent
yelping, a screaming at the grass
—living record of soil's
nourishment, oracle of what-will-be.
That little bat, flying mouse, cut down,
scooped up, driven to sanctuary, over
mountains and beneath cathedral trees
in a lovingly padded shoebox.
Rescued from and for nothing.
Anesthetized, burned, destroyed and
deposited without ceremony beneath
headstone blades of green on the
wrong side of the Pacific Coast Range.

YOUNG'N

The juvenile gull—
a western, I think—
likely came in the hope
of claiming some flung morsel.
Or maybe it was to share
our space after all,
for in the absence of food
it lowered itself to the belly
and the blowing sand
began to pile and sculpt itself
against our forms.

No sooner had it buried its head to sleep
than we looked to each other
then thanked the gull for the moment
in low whispers.
It, too young to know better
than to trust.
We, old enough to know better
than to stay so long, uncovered and burnt,
sharing, too, those hours
with the sun.

DAHLIA

the petal gateway
electric in its emissions
takes more than I give
and I know
you are as alive with it as I am

GENUFLECTION #2

On the crushed gravel trail
you swatted flies
spat about saints
all the while questing
for my allegiance
to Holy Truth

I did not say it:
that no person is always holy
nor wholly good

Instead I knelt before the
distant swallow and
ground-covered fieldmouse
bent a servile left knee
to their perfect simplicity

An altar boy drunk
on the blood
of tailed and wingéd christs

NIGHT CHORUS

Chorus frogs count
the seconds in rounds which
stumble, stutter over one another.
The television's mute glow
is losing its anemic fight
with the wall
above two snoring dogs
and a formless blanket betrays
the shape of a graceful frame;
your body curled,
fingers clasped together,
in prayer to the Sandman
and his ilk.
You and they,
he and his,
dreamers all.

BIRD CHORUS
(after Euripides' *The Bird-Choros of Ion*)

blood-stained songbird
blossom thief
whistling undaunted
in her labors
flees with petals
in crimsoned beak
to holy, wave-swept Kinneret

A SONG OF WASTELANDS

There are wastes where
folk march single file
through shrubs and scotch broom
where old growth cedar
used to count bare-ground
winters by the tens and hundreds

Or where men and women
unsheltered sit on concrete
and ask for love or time
or simple eye contact
getting none from betters who
leave them in frigid wakes

A wasteland too
where a man looks past the door
to watch her sleep
mustering the courage to
climb into bed or else
stay put to think
on what he'll say tomorrow
at the end of it all.

LEAFFOOTED BUG

I see you, you leaf-footed thing.
Astride cool metal,
featureless metal,
antennae probing for tomato scent
or squash.
What you're doing in my airport,
I'm sure, is beyond us both.

To put you out in the rain
At the PDX terminal
(a clause as synthetic,
manmade and garish as your
current alloyed surface)
may be, perhaps, to put you to death.
To leave you here
at departures, equally so.
It's up to me.

I've moved twice now,
and twice you've shifted
your ambling, discerning
gait toward my place,
toward me. Toward fate.
So we'll go outside.
Maybe there, at least,
you'll find something discarded
to stave off the end.

HARUKI ON THE BEACH

sand and sedge of the dune
consume the periphery
a choir of grit and tiny blades

behind me in the ocean
where close up
breaking waves whisper
a pelican smacks the water after
some humming morsel behind
that whale breaching every few minutes
to shout about salt
at the vaster blue above her
silent and invisible

behind me the ocean
and I at the base of my dune
facing sand and sedge wallpaper
am reading a novel by Murakami
haunted Japanese man
and everything back there
is fit only to drone and murmur
and pass through the sieve

a formless white soundscape
atop which float
all his strangled quiet words

THE NINTH CIRCLE

he became as a god
when he lost the heater
for the koi pond out back
to the February snow
when the water turned mostly solid
and he hammered a pipe
down three feet to check
discovering he'd
condemned his fish
to the ninth circle of hell
all cold and black
cold and black

ROO BOY

His breath is shallow at the end
but still he issues lungfuls of intent.
Half-lidded eyes looking
toward the prospect of rest.
Maybe something more.

The weight of my hand comes
to rest on his nape
and his tail thumps just once, firm,
a love greater than I've earned,
but there it is, reaching through
all that old, tired pain.

BANDED AGATE

Bands of cream and silver wrapped themselves
around it, golden and warm as honey.

It tumbled there beneath breaking waves,
threatened to roll back out and down forever

if I didn't plunge in, lunge after it then and there
without hesitation or thought of the swift current

and water, colder than any bold shower I've taken.
Worth it for such vibrant treasure. Worth it even now

after finding that it wasn't the finest specimen
after all, its bands fewer than I first realized,

less regular, then not at all. But I grasped after it still
and found its smoothness wasn't exactly that;

in one of its tiny potholes was a gray pebble
lodged firm, gazing out like some fossilized cataract

from this stone, heart-shaped at a certain angle
but more like a sick kidney from all other vantages.

I realized, too it wasn't golden but green, and that a
trick of light had transmuted pale and gasping jasper

in a false instant of wet sun flashing over a form
still wanting, still set to wait another hundred years

to achieve that marble sheen and rounded beauty
that only a moment ago thoroughly willed into being,

so perfectly pretended, until I had it in my hand.
But I'm sure, certain, that I grabbed the right one.

VACCINIUM PARVIFOLIUM

Time spent picking red huckleberries
is best lent toward inward thought.
Appreciation of quiet,
contemplating mortality.

They grow from the dead, you know—
sprung from rotting wood and acid soil,
they resist, no, reject cultivation.
It's only the Mother who grows them
with consistency from her fallen, wooden children.
In reverence for these sacrifices,
red huckleberry grows urn-shaped flowers:
tokens of memory and gratitude
for the rot from which they rise.
How appropriate
that the fruit is bittersweet.
And so you have to want them;
as you have to wait for their coming,
resign yourself to their size.

Too sparse to grasp by the handful,
they are to be plucked, one-by-one,
sometimes in pairs–rarely threes,
if you find a shrub especially lush
and are greedy.
Firm and perfect rounds
leap away at the smallest bounce–
leaf to hand, hand to jar.

If I had before me
the multitude of red huckleberries
that have escaped my grasp in life
I could bake one. Whole. Pie.

For those who know, that's no trifling number,
those many that found their way down.
But I don't want them back. Those seeds
are my tokens of memory and gratitude
for that space. For this place.

LEAN BACK YOUR HEAD

Lean back your head,
and rest it,
stare up
at what you will.
Now, fingers ready,
write out a few
syllables.
List a few words
describing your
earliest vibrant
childhood memory.
Now some old
deep hurt.
Give them an
object to share
if you will.
Think on it hard
(or don't).
Picture your face:
unaged, selfsame.
Body trembling,
fists clenched.
Or the back of
your skull aching
from laughter.
Feel the weight.
Try not to cry.

Or do.
What shape is it all?
Feel the sharp corners,
trace the rounds
and gently press
your fingertips into
the soft parts inside it.
You're a poet.

URNS

When my mother's mother Suzie
died in my fourteenth year
I didn't cry
I wanted to
I remember being perplexed
frustrated at the failure
I did cry later but
only from shame
for not doing so
where and when

My mother well and grown
is an orphan now

I eventually tattooed Suzie's
memory and that shame on
my wrist in the form of
Gene Stratton Porter's honeybee
I kiss it sometimes
kiss holy Grandma

When my father's father died
his name was Jim
I cried wept
really wept
it was not from the loss
but an adult empathy
for my fatherless father
for my future self

perhaps as well
no tattoo but I wrote poems
and my ears pray now as my
mouth and mind could never do
to my grandfather's vinyl records

I stare sometimes at the bee
while listening to old spinning vinyl

Why didn't I share in my
mother's impossible loss
that absence of a saintly
woman yet marked it
forever onto my body
to remember and love?

Why did I cry for my father
but not for his own
that gentle-man who spoke in
stories and smiles
in weather and kind words?

THE MAN HIMSELF

So many inchoate
movements, kindled
with burning words
to incipient hoards—
even if they collapse
into themselves leaving
only smoke, brittle and stale—
give out parts, singly
and in droves, to the multitudes,
countless her- and his-own tragic
and glorious and pointless plays,
prophesied one and all by
a man of no small wit.

for Walt Whitman

I BET YOU CAN'T HIT ME
WITH A QUARTER

Standing there with his cardboard
sign, he shuddered visibly under diagonal
rain. Our conversation in the car
stuttered. Both of us burning with the
desire to help, fearful to engage, apprehensive
at his maybe-mental (or chemical) state.

Instinctively, my hand rested on my lap,
covering the hip pocket. Her arms crossed to
guard and safeguard at once.
His eyes pulled at the rain, pushed it
hard into our windshield to label, hiss
the names of our fears, shames, sympathies,
conjoined selfishness.

Is there a word for that scene?
What is the name for that emotional niche
which the rain tried so vainly,
so angrily to pronounce on his behalf?

FROM IN THE DUST CLOUD

Behind the combines—
churning rows of uniform
decay—rise clouds full of rust
and wheezing churning
swallowing vomiting
a hundred two hundred
years worth of Sunday best
of small town values
of fear and xenophobia
fashion all heavy boots
and canvas and leather
and blood just itching
for a fight in the corner
highway bar or for absolution
from the confessional or
from the lap of a woman
with work-roughed hands
but only after too-late change
comes and anger churns
latent fears or after
a loved one steps beyond
the veil from this to next
and words or actions or both
take on their own rusted hue
of hate or blood
or pernicious argument
cemented by months years

decades of walled silence
into heartbreak and sometimes
that dark crossroads climbs
over the horizon in minutes
hours or days but takes
a seeming fullness of time
to make itself known

Madison County, IN

WHEN IT'S TIME

When it's time
to put away the things
which made me burn
once, full of faith and joy,
I know it's because
I've learned and breathed
too much in spaces
where self-deprivation
and shame or wounds
of an apocryphal, holy nature
on some head and hands
and feet and ribs
offer no reward, have nothing
to do with owning and accounting
for simple human failure,
nothing to share with regret
for the sake of itself,
nothing to rise and meet
the elation felt when others
danced and sang
on top of moss and beneath
dripping fir trees simply
for the excuse to do so.

THE LABOR TEMPLE

Fridays here are Tuesdays now.
They say it's different—devoid of the old Work Ethic:
the Labor Temple. Astoria.
The summer swell of tourists elevates the Temple
filling its seats for a while with lip gloss,
karaoke, idle minds.
Come November the Temple will sink
back toward the sea, in time,
a damp and whimpled return to past and namesake.

It was a temple, real.
A blue-collar high priest tended bar.
It *was* one back then. Prayers
from bowed heads fell into pints and highballs
for nearly a century here onto oiled wood
polished by so many hands and elbows.
How many didn't even feel the need to whisper—

Nurses, teachers, tellers, clerks,
loggers, fishermen, artisans, clergymen.
Tired mothers and fathers.

They knew what work was but if you asked
they wouldn't tell you
because you didn't deserve to know.
They knew a budget isn't a balanced checkbook.

It was in your pocket
your flimsy wallet storing sweat-softened bills
designated with no small regard
for cheap beer and whiskey
at the Temple (or some similar place of worship).

They labored and between times
came to the Temple to pray.

Astoria, OR

NEEDLE/NAVEL

As through a pillow,
the tinny voice falls
backward, smothered.
Lost luster, from a veil
of cotton or polyester or hair.
And, unlike the lint
plucked daily from my navel
(which I always wish I'd saved
over the years for a
cringe-worthy someday-sweater),
my fingers adopt a delicacy
and care not mustered before,
to remove the fuzz
from the turntable's needle.
Then, Michael Hurley, singing true,
tells me some more
about the hound and the whale
and nighttime creatures.

OLD GOAT

Old goat,
nothing shall take you.
Your curious gaze,
demon's eyes,
amphibian's eyes,
a lover's eyes—
Mark of Cain—
our hopes and
our anxieties,
balanced and opposed,
on horizontal scales forged
on ancient Hydra
and quenched in her
long-dead springs.

PHOENIX BY WAY OF PORTLAND

A great cylinder hums, thrums, surrounds.
Full of shallow breaths,
and the electricity of tight chests.
To either side, wide flat angles, stretching.

It feels more romantic to say,
"Somewhere out there, there
is such and such happening,"
doesn't it?
As if it were said by someone *down there*.

Somewhere out there
a great cylinder vibrates with energy,
electricity and anxiety.

It screams at the distant horizon
with mountain lungs
and the breath of low winter sun.

When the portal finally opens,
living cargo gulps dry air and sniffles
at the memory of high altitude.
But there is no hugging damp,
no vapor to cling to
in the Fire Bird's city.

SAGAN DALYA

There they are:
leaves drifting listless
in a steel sink.
A kind of rhododendron,
not at all the same
as the toxic variety blooming
in arboreal chains along
this north coast.

"Sagan Dalya" in Buryat.

What an obscure bit of nature
to have infiltrated my damp
sea-blown cottage, and so
distant from its home among
high and arid and rocky soils.

How strange to be so dislocated.
How tragic to travel so far
finally to arrive, only to drown
as refuse in a basin
crowded by so much cold
glass and indifferent gray water.

HAYSTACKS

Recently I dreamed of killing my father.
More than once, actually,
and just once he tried to end me.
I cannot find the why of it.
It's a needle...
He is so kind. I wish
that we were closer.

My hair is thinning already.
I'm not even halfway done living
(God willing).
Thinning, and my beard
is lighter than it's ever been.
A few white strands frost my jaw.
Almost becoming my father's jaw.

A few miles down the coast
basalt rock formations jut up
from the heaving water, their great
haystack bodies rooted fast to the earth,
immovable, seemingly permanent,
alike in disposition and makeup,
huddled close to one another.

EUROPEAN STARLINGS ABOVE ASTORIA

Singular motion, built from multitudes, turning thick,
to near-vanishing lace and foam and back again.
And that wisp of urgent few who missed the turn of
the mass behind them, surging toward the falling sun,
banking in luxury, witness the sudden gap. The panic
of being outside the rhythm sends them winging
backward, shouting to rejoin their joyful murmuration
and the holy mass resumes; A lullaby for the city
below. A Slow, drowsing, viscous tumble. Choir-wave
of five thousand voices, a tide which has long since
traded the driving moon for gentle dusk. Hardly less
ancient, no less cleansing, as pure or purer than that
distant cold stone, than its white, soft light.

RAINFALL, 10PM

And those thousand heavy drops
smacking deck boards are typing
in layered drumroll and singing in rounds
the Word that stretches into predawn gray,
impossible to pronounce as it is never finished
but only pauses, fades and leaps again
into this hour, the next, into tomorrow, six days
hence, its meaning universal—all things rolled
together. Time and slumber. Secrets.
The music of tree frogs.
A roosting barnswallow back from migration
and the ennui that must set in after such a trip.
The changing tilt of the earth.
It is you there and me here.

KITCHEN ANTS

Questing ever for food. Perhaps a drink of water
We all need it and, like us, they seem to prefer it
in a glass to a puddle, droplet or a dirty dish.

It's a small intelligence they have, presumably,
but with so many cooperative facets.
Emergent, even, in some Other way.

I won't poison them; vinegar is a fine deterrent.
But the north coast winter rains drive them
indoors from cold and flooding soils.

Fine then. Let them warm their little bodies.
There's nothing to be done about winter.
For now, at this moment, they are housemates.

But when I find them, in my salad, bananas
or cereal bowl, I'll rescind this offer. They'll stay,
but not without some choice four-letter words.

DRIVING WITH LEONARD COHEN

I'm leaning with the curves in the road
pushing through marine layer mist in a car
dotted with its usual assortment of litter:

A disused phone charger
wrapped around the gearshift.
The vacant water bottle needing a good scrub.
Sand and fur on the floors and in the small spaces
from beach visits with the dogs. Gum wrappers...

Everything as usual but for my quiet, well-dressed
passenger watching the sand and surf scroll past his
window. When he finally speaks his voice is deep,
richer than I expect: a hand smoothing rumpled
velvet, but running against the grain.

He's just let out a few dry syllables
and punctuates the air with half a grin
before settling back into silence.

I grin too, so wide that the space behind my ears
warms and tightens into a tension headache.
It almost feels like prayer.

We've never met, but his death hasn't stopped him
joining me on the floor late at night with spinning
vinyl, in margins of notebooks, or on gray-green
drives at the edge of the sea.

CATHEDRAL TOWN

Astoria is a cathedral town
container ships face east
with the incoming tide
great alcoveless churches
rose windows watching
and biding river-time for the
Second Coming
or for port of entry
to be granted upstream
whichever comes first

WITCH'S WOOD

I'll trade you the dreams
of a sleeping dog
for the first full view
of the rising Harvest moon.
Then we can all twitch
happily beneath it—
you, the dog, and I
under pale and ghostly light
in dance of one sort or another.

Clatsop State Forest, OR

TAR PAPER

Next door needs work. The neighbors are doing it,
but it's their second home, or third.
Either way, no hurry.
But it rained all day today and now the tar paper
beneath the eave facing my house is sagging
like the dress of a woman with two drinks too many,
and whose one wild breast lolls carelessly
over the drooping fabric, neither she
nor the exposed flesh aware—
or maybe it's just that neither cares.
In any case, this is no weather for a quarter-finished
remodel to just sit.

Back in the trees about a mile from my door
are some number of strangers.
How many I can't say, but they sleep
beneath mildewed blankets and ripped tarpaulin.
Earlier we saw two ambulances
speed up to the Goodwill store
and park out back where paramedics
situated themselves to deliver aid
to victims of overdose or other trauma
and whisked them from the camp to the hospital.
We were there to browse puzzles and books,
seeking occupation to pass the storm
inside our four walls, under
the sturdy roof of home.

BARN SWALLOW

I don't know the sex of it or its age.
The partner is a little more drab
so maybe it's a "he".
How far his migration was I can't know.
Nor how many eggs may be in the nest,
if there are any at all. I won't check.

But I know, even without hearing
through this closed window,
by seeing his vibration, his humming.
That small movement and quivering tail.
That percolating throat.

He's a miniature feathered kettle
approaching full boil, signaling
readiness for the day,
all that warbled chatter steaming forth
To greet the sun.

THREE POEMS AND A MOUNTAIN

A small place. A large place.
Where I do not fit but have landed,
we are small and large at once, or so I've read.
Our being is and is and is, or so it is said.

Here, in a nook of the trembling landscape
where hills push up and back, away from
the crying ocean whose breath is wind,
She looks to her older Rocky cousins.
But it is no less, the Mystery here,
than in those high, sparse places to the biting east.
Lush, green and primordial, but eternally young,
somehow, too. She sings.

The Beastly Mound, thing of hunched shoulders
settled into nightly mist and clothed with
weeping cedar and fir, gathering air and memory.
The Low-High Place: Neah-Kah-Nie.

Neahkahnie Mountain, OR

WAGONER'S SHOE

I wish only to be some lesser part
of David Wagoner or Barry Lopez.
No—I would be the gum on their shoes
and, even though,
like Wagoner and Lopez and Root,
I have traversed the land
from midwest to west and settled
in dim corners and bright corners,
I have yet to lose myself in Barry's two landscapes,
the inner-mind and outer-place.

Where was it I was planning to go so urgent and wide
that I haven't yet been?
For the life of me, I can't remember.
My start was someplace so far back—I sit now,
lost and small.
The piece of gum.
The pebble in the sole's tread.
A realization that has yet to come forward,
to make it to some larger space.

So I'll sit here a while until I spot that thrush whistling
upward in spirals and dripping soft like the red
cedar's tears after rain until some motion or notion
takes me by the nape and thrusts my senses,
toward the scent of it coming
down the Columbia toward the Pacific.
Down the Tippecanoe toward the Wabash in Indiana,
down into the distant Mississippi delta.

POETRY WITH CHUCK

sifting through notes and discussing our Favorites
looking for traces of them
at the bottom of a whiskey bottle

or in a bowl of tuna poke
amongst the grain of turned wood

in the interstices we hammer out lines
on a vintage _____ typewriter (what was it?)

with a long view of the sunset
the bay
the river
and its ribbon
of traffic ruining the orange glass surface at a slant

trying to pin down clouds as a song said somewhere
typing writing seeking drinking after Mystery

Q: Why, during their migration, is one half of the
geese's V always larger?

A: Simple: there are just more birds on that side.

FLINT/TENDER

Stepping over tilled frozen rows,
dirt crunching like ten-degree snow,
snubs of corn stalks like tombstones,
like soldiers, like Arlington,
shrinking away in every direction.
Death is only a few months old here.

And here, too, a piece older by far—
triangle flint with a notched base. Any blood
it drew or beast it felled at least
a century gone.
Any blood, sweat or viscera
that's hit the ground here since
is only figurative or caused, very real,
by the cutter bar of a combine.

Cold toes that turn to hot turn to drumbeat throbbing.
A mile to get back before checking
any damage already etched in.
Pick up the pace, see it sooner,
but see it just the same,
unchanged, no less done.

Warsaw, IN

FISHER POET #1

rough-edged man, rhyming untrained
with only so many syllables per word.
the fewer the better...
line after line after line,
the Fisher-Poet washes over his crowd,
wave action incarnate,
wearing loud the salt of his skin,
rank fish oil and the sea's sweat.
he pulls them in a little at a time
no hurry at all yet straining all the while.

2023 Fisher Poets Gathering, Astoria, OR

FISHER POET #2

windblown woman, your knuckles are white
as the pages in your work-rasped hands,

wading through your recitation with a chant, shifting
to a dirge and finally to a work song. then back.

back again across the order pitching
and heaving in slow motion
like the tide cycle,
complete with your spittle of surfspray,

with the dead and living things cast up
or pulled from depths
which, you say, give us much
but can take so much more.

2023 Fisher Poets Gathering, Astoria, OR

SOU'WESTER, SEAVIEW, WA

Sou'wester Lodge; temporary home to creatives
and stolid types alike.
Grab a turntable, records from the vinyl library
(honor system—be good).

Lean on the outdoor kitchen bar,
with its polished live-edge, an amber river
in the morning sun, its knots all silent boulders
beneath a mirror-pond surface.

Sip on Thundermuck,
coffee so strong and smoky
it's a liquid lumberjack.

Now go back to the spot you picked. That tiny
airstream. That renovated Bluebird bus,

Or any other of the custom, varied vintage campers,
so many repurposed into strange, new, useful spaces.
Recording studio, tea room, movie theater...

Cubbies to fit your style and tastes, named just so:
Aristocrat.
Potato Bug.
Prairie Schooner.
African Queen.

DIRGE, SEAVIEW, WA

On a dune trail today
I made the sign of the cross
(a latent reflex from a time
when the priesthood called)

as a Coast Guard helicopter
made low, slow passes
over my Ocean God just past
the Columbia River bar:
Graveyard of the Pacific.

A pang of loss and pity
for some missing soul
an ant in a cauldron
praying to angry stormwater
for the smallest mercy.

I left the rain to write,
to listen to the rotor blades
as I sat by a heater
praying after a fashion
and sipping on warm words.

UPLAND

There's a restoration project at the bottom of Bear
Creek, before its confluence with the Columbia,
where beavers took the Plumas Sitka Willow stand,
left the fir and spruce to greater appetites
(like those great timber vessels awaiting port of entry
up in Longview and beyond).

A dipper was mapping Gnat Creek on my last visit,
flying low along its contours, taking them down
rather than the straight shot upstream
I watched, squatting, while she secreted breaths
of morning knowledge beneath riffles, under stones,
in exchange for Caddisfly larvae, river snails and fry.

Higher up, where these streams are smaller—
diluting themselves into a hundred creeklets and
rivulets— they are overseen by fern-hill chanterelle
nurseries, duff scent and aromas of pepper and
apricot, choirs of angles and slopes
about the quiet ways of being.

UNDER THERE
for William Pitt Root

Water like a drum
thrums at the river's edge.

Look up, out, at the thousand peaks
frothing white atop
the rounded seascape.
A ways out, a boat hovers.

No chart marks this blemish.

Who else may be out there
in the murk, watching the land?
Do like minds move under all that
heaving wave action?

WILD MAN

He runs marathons.
Long gray hair trailing
and a grinning beard might wrap
sideways around his chin
with the right wind.
Everyone in his orbit
has been given a nickname,
each a close-enough
acquaintance to be called "friend".

Once, asked at the starting line
why he always kicks off at such speed,
such a white-hot pace, he hooted:
"TO STAY AHEAD OF DEATH!"
and, cackling, bounded forth.

Joy with a punchline,
vibrating with light,
holy in his way.

DIRT BATH

dust from the trail in its feathers
the sparrow shoulders-in deep
ruffle-scatters
motes of the path
      and then
when the thought of flight takes hold
casts heavenward
pinpricks of earth

Fort to Sea Trail, Lewis & Clark Natl. Historic Park

HYPOXIA

Walt Whitman
prophesied it best:
"Bathe the land, mankind,
in nutritive cocktails. Grow!"

Water comes alive,
green and thick with algae.
But watch it die.
And with the rot
goes the oxygen.

Underwater creatures
drowning en masse
(who've no business doing so).
Predators and prey alike
starve or leave or vanish.
Marine deserts appear.

Now see, too, livelihoods wither.
Livelihoods of those who
took more than enough
from Nature to begin with.

Tragedy (or maybe justice,
depending on who you ask, and
about whom you speak).

Just don't ask the fish
the crustaceans
the marine mammals
or anyone frustrated
by supermarket hikes
on frozen shrimp.

A PONCA MAN ON THE LEFT COAST
for Cliff Taylor

There is a Ponca man on the left coast.
who is writing joyfully
about ancestors, the Little People,
and his big-footed Brother of the wild.
One of many fusing the past
with the present, with the future.
More of this.

After a season of cold and darkness
the first buds of Spring quicken.
Tender packets of energy
from that which only looked, to some, to be gone.

AND THE MOMENTS

turned to sameness,
jasper pebbles tumbled
beneath waves, surf-shaped
and smoothed to identical rounds,
each and next and next
indistinguishable, one from another.

BROKEN POET

You are. So go ahead and drink
your melancholy wine, howl like you do
at dreams and shadows, and rage quietly, late,
over the bitter echoes
of your lost, strange, absent power.
Give yourself permission:
mourn the loss of your imagination but don't let go
of the brittle admissions
before you. Hold them up:
Coward. Imposter. Grown and still lost.

EDEN, INDIANA

Not the unincorporated township.

I stumbled into Eden south of Pisgah Marsh:
honeysuckle, pawpaw, honey bees, woodcocks.
Even a skunk, who simply trotted off a ways.
This land used to be wetland;
there must be a spring here somewhere.

I say, "used to be" like the soil, the geology,
the hydrology—landscape's soul—
don't all still make it so.
But it was drained for farms
in the late nineteenth century. The twentieth
gave almost eighty percent the state's land
as a dowry to Big Ag.

Still, these holy places persist.
Some bits are dedicated, like Pisgah: tokens
to soothe the modern West that lives
on the homes and histories of older cultures.

Others, like this place...a border
grass lane between tax lots, guarding
a wellspring and singing green joys,
bright and buzzing—the air rarefied
though low.
Sanctity in liminal space,
in spite of everything.

THE DREAM

We are back at St. Mary's,
in the old kindergarten room.
Eight or so of us divide up the psilocybin mushrooms
that I have smuggled in here in my pocket.
Somehow, Mr. Lynch attends, strict disciplinarian,
and he is into it. Did he take some, too?
We wander around my old neighborhood.
"There are still five hours before school lets out,"
someone says. We take in the sunshine.
A stork in a blue sweater and black tights
is walking through the sky, her wing rowing
like Michael Jordan flying from the free throw line.
You find some of your old, beloved potted plants
(in the yard of my childhood home, though you
grew up hours north of here, impossibly far away)
and move them into the sun,
because *fuck those people*
for not taking better care of them.
When too many of the others try to visit with us,
all on their own trips, not reading our room,
we walk off to talk (or not talk)—
I with my pen and notebook,
you with something sacred of your own.
What is it?

POKING AROUND IN MAY

There is still ice on the trails
where the sun can't quite settle in

but only makes dappled pools
of quickened, bitter cold.

Wisened moss and lichen pull it in,
extend themselves along the edge

of the worn footpath. On the many
interstices between man- and nature-made

as if there is a difference, as if
we are separated from it all

between boulder and fern and
along the shaded places, on rotting

life-giving nurse logs. They rest
and make my poke all the more perilous

for having to sidestep, stop
short and reach with feet, past balance

to avoid these and other tender, precious forms
of newts and slugs, assassin bugs questing.

GEORGE

Not my grandfather
but may as well have been.
Gave me a book of jokes from the '30s
racist caricatures disguised as humor.

Even so young it tilted me had me
asking what-that-word-means.
I threw it out, but not before
crawling through just a few more pages.

Poured for me that first bitter cup
of coffee, the sweet burn of brandy.
Passed me a knife as big as my forearm.
We would visit plenty through the years
always, almost always, talking

about passenger jets and cargo ships.
I sent sporadic pictures like lightning
through the air a continent away
of vessels lined up on the Columbia.

After he left for good at ninety-three
I was given a colorless photograph
from his navy days: Jeans, chambray
and that too-white dixie cup hat
almost glowing in the monochrome.

FLOORMUTTS

When they curl their paws, these two old dogs,
while tails thump the floor and breathing slows,
deepens to move in time with huffs and snorts
in punctuated rhythm, I picture for them
what I Imagine to be a glorious day,
one for the books:

For her it's a little dog—the size she loves—
to chase on the sand, and that squirrel
that almost got away (almost being the best part).
Close, but no cigar, Mr. Squirrel.
That last bit I grant to her, if only in this exercise.

For him the beach, too, with its washed up and
picked-over crab legs, delectable rotting scents,
a tennis ball to retrieve again and again before
settling onto a hardier chew toy for the drive home.

Then comes dinner. Oh, dinner. And dessert (which
is the cats' dinner). Then naps, long and plush
on beds that I'd sleep on myself, have done.

I picture it all because of course I can't know,
but it's on these days, with all the aforementioned,
when they snore and thump and huff and twitch
their whiskers, curl their paws,
that I figure they are replaying memories
from what I hope has been the Good Life.

CHANTERELLE FOR MENG HAORAN[1]

Step lightly, soft, over trillium
Reach beneath the sword fern

Lift its arm to see little sister
Spring chanterelle greeting the day

---

[1] Meng Haoran was a Tang Dynasty Sanshui (landscape) poet who lived during the late 7th and 8th centuries. His poems used simple, conversational language that looked to the natural world. What a guy.

ACKNOWLEDGMENTS

To Broken Tribe Press for bringing this manuscript to realization: thank you for your time and care.

Special thanks, too, go to the folks at Plan B Press, who took a chance on my first poetry chapbook, *Here, in the Floodplain*. A handful of those poems are a part of this collection.

My thanks also to the following publications, in which some of these titles, or versions of them, first appeared: *The Elevation Review* (Kneeland Center for Poetry); *The North Coast Squid* (Hoffman Center for the Arts); *Flying Island* (the Indiana Writers Center); *The Salal Review* (Lower Columbia College); and *The Upper Left Edge*, and the Neahkahnie Mountain Poetry Prize (Hoffman Center for the Arts) for my poem 5 *November*, also a part of this collection.

To poet, lepidopterist and man-of-the-world, Dr. Robert Michael Pyle, for pulling me out of the vacuum and into a writing community, for providing both friendship and mentorship along the way, and for helping me to render this manuscript into something worth reading.

Last but most—Thank you, Vanessa, for always supporting this quiet and inward pursuit with all your joy.

CREDITS

MEZUZAH - *The North Coast Squid* (2023)

HERE, IN THE FLOODPLAIN - *The Elevation Review* (2022), Plan B Press (2023)

HATCHET MAN - *The Elevation Review* (2022), Plan B Press (2023)

5 NOVEMBER - *Neahkahnie Mountain Poetry Prize*, Hoffman Center for the Arts (2023)

BLUE LIGHT - Plan B Press (2023)

HARUKI ON THE BEACH - Plan B Press (2023)

THE LABOR TEMPLE - Plan B Press (2023)

NEEDLE/NAVEL - Plan B Press (2023)

PHOENIX BY WAY OF PORTLAND - Plan B Press (2023)

SAGAN DALYA - *Flying Island Journal* (2023)

THREE POEMS AND A MOUNTAIN - *The Upper Left Edge* (2023)

WITCH'S WOOD - *The Salal Review* (2024)

TELEOLOGY OF THE SOIL – *Broken Tribe Review* (2024)

ABOUT THE AUTHOR

Logan Garner is a Hoosier/PNW poet residing on Oregon's north coast. Winner of the Neahkahnie Mountain Poetry Prize, his work has been featured in *Orca Literary Journal, The Elevation Review, The Salal Review, Flying Island, Broken Tribe Review,* and others, as well as Tupelo Press's 30/30 project in 2024. He is also the author of collection *Here, in the Floodplain* (Plan B Press, 2023).